DATE DUE

PRINTED IN U.S.A.

Endangered and Extinct ANIMALS OF THE ISLANDS AND OCEANS

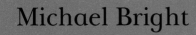

Michael Bright

Copper Beech Books
Brookfield, Connecticut

© Aladdin Books Ltd 2002

Produced by:
Aladdin Books Ltd
28 Percy Street
London W1P 0LD

ISBN 0–7613–2711–8

*First published in the
United States in 2002 by:*
Copper Beech Books,
an imprint of
The Millbrook Press
2 Old New Milford Road
Brookfield, Connecticut 06804

Editor:
Kathy Gemmell

Designer:
Flick, Book Design & Graphics

Illustrators:
Tim Bramfitt, Dave Burroughs,
Darren Harvey, Peter Hayman,
Gary Hincks, Ian Jackson
(Wildlife Art), Mick Loates,
Alan Male, Sean Milne,
Francis Phillipps, John Rignall,
Rob Shone, Ian Thompson,
Simon Turvey (Wildlife Art),
Phil Weare, Maurice Wilson
Cartoons: Jo Moore

Certain illustrations have
appeared in earlier books
created by Aladdin Books.

Cataloging-in-Publication
data is on file at the
Library of Congress.

Contents

Introduction

Even in the vastness of the world's oceans, animals are not safe from the influence of humans. Many fish and some species of deep-sea sharks are being overfished. Oil slicks kill seabirds and mammals, plastic trash is found floating in the middle of the ocean, and poisonous wastes are found in the tissues of animals even in the remotest ocean depths. Islands were once isolated, but every one that has been visited by people has been damaged in some way. Many island plants and animals have been driven to extinction. Our oceans and islands are under threat.

Q: Why watch for these boxes?

A: For answers to the animal questions you always wanted to ask.

zoom in on...

Bits and pieces

These boxes take a closer look at the features of certain animals or issues.

Awesome facts

Watch for these dodo diamonds to learn more about the weird and wonderful facts on endangered and extinct animals and their world.

Endangered and extinct

When few animals of a particular species survive in the wild, it is said to be endangered. If a species disappears altogether, it is extinct. Some extinctions are caused by human activities. Others are caused by natural events, like changes in climate or sea level, or competition from similar animals.

SYMBOL DEFINITIONS
In this book, the red cross symbol shows an animal that is already extinct. The yellow exclamation shows an animal that is endangered. Animals that are less endangered are said to be "vulnerable." Those that are more endangered and close to extinction are said to be "critically endangered." The green tick shows an animal that has either been saved from the brink of extinction or has recently been discovered. Many of these "success" stories, however, are still endangered species.

Mamo

Green turtle

Sea otter

Animals that have been introduced into a particular habitat, accidentally or on purpose, are called alien animals. Cats, for example, are taken by humans to islands where they do not occur naturally. If they breed, they attack and kill the resident animals and can cause them to become extinct.

Q: Does it matter if some animals become extinct?

A: Yes. Every plant and animal on Earth is important. Each has its role to play in the natural order. Removing one upsets the order and affects other living things. The overall picture of life on Earth—the variety of plants and animals, their behavior, and the ways in which they interact—is called biodiversity. Maintaining biodiversity is essential for the survival of all species.

Many species of ocean and island animals were plentiful until people arrived. Birds that had adapted to life on isolated islands were easy prey for sailors looking for food. Many became extinct soon after people first arrived. Great auks (above) used to nest in tens of millions on rocky North Atlantic coasts, but by 1844 they had been hunted to extinction.

The preservation of an animal's living space is critical for its survival. If its habitat is destroyed, it has nowhere to live and nothing to eat. Coral reefs are rich in marine animal life. They get clogged up by oil slicks and by mud washed off the land. They are also under threat from tourists and from fishermen who use dynamite to catch fish. When a reef is harmed, its animal life disappears and it takes hundreds of years to recover, if at all.

Ocean giants

During the 19th and 20th centuries, whales were almost wiped out from the world's oceans by the whaling industry. By 1986, most species were on the brink of extinction and whaling nations voted to end commercial whaling. Whale populations gradually began to recover.

Q: Who makes sure too many whales aren't killed?

A: A "club" of whaling nations, known as the International Whaling Commission (IWC). Each year, the members debate restarting whaling, but pressure from antiwhaling nations and from conservation organizations like Greenpeace encourages most nations to conserve whales and not kill them.

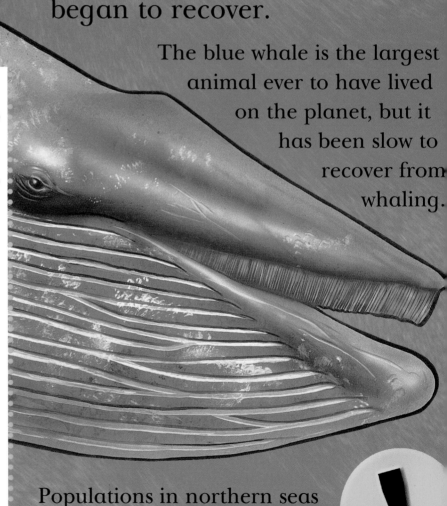

The blue whale is the largest animal ever to have lived on the planet, but it has been slow to recover from whaling.

Populations in northern seas are growing, but those in the Southern Ocean are still low.

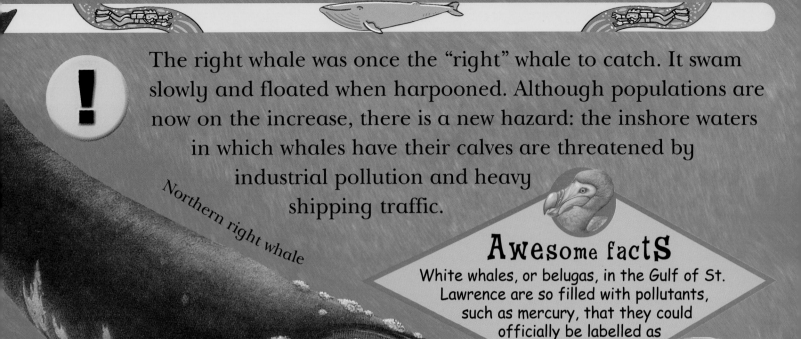

The right whale was once the "right" whale to catch. It swam slowly and floated when harpooned. Although populations are now on the increase, there is a new hazard: the inshore waters in which whales have their calves are threatened by industrial pollution and heavy shipping traffic.

Northern right whale

Awesome factS

White whales, or belugas, in the Gulf of St. Lawrence are so filled with pollutants, such as mercury, that they could officially be labelled as "toxic waste."

Zoom in on...

"Scientific" whaling

Some whaling nations have sidestepped the whaling ban by killing whales, such as minke whales in the Southern Ocean, with the excuse that they are taken for "scientific purposes." However, the meat is sold in the usual way in the market.

The vaquita is a porpoise and the smallest relative of whales and dolphins. It lives in the Gulf of California, where it is often drowned in fishing nets or poisoned by pollutants. A high casualty rate has made it the rarest porpoise in the world.

Vaquita porpoise

7

zoom in on...

Monk seals

Monk seals are the most primitive seals. The Caribbean monk seal (right) was hunted for its oil and hide and was last seen in 1952, off Jamaica. It is now thought to be extinct. Other monk seals survive, but are critically endangered. They are easily disturbed by boats and will often abandon their pups.

X

Awesome facts
The Caribbean monk seal was the first New World mammal spotted and logged by Christopher Columbus when he crossed the Atlantic Ocean in 1492.

Seals and sea cows

Seals, sea lions, and sea cows were heavily killed for their blubber, meat, and hide. Northern elephant seals, which breed on the Pacific coast of the U.S., were almost wiped out by early sealers. A hunting ban has led to the recovery of the seals and of their main predator, the great white shark.

All sea cows today, including manatees (right) and dugongs, were once hunted for their meat. Today, entanglement in fishing nets, pollution, and injury from boat propellers are their major threats.

Steller's sea cow

Steller's sea cow was discovered in 1740, but exterminated 27 years later. It was hunted ruthlessly because its fat burned with a clear flame and its meat was delicious. German naturalist Georg Steller was the only scientist to see it alive and describe it to other scientists.

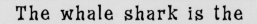

The great white shark has killed more people than any other shark, but most attacks are thought to be cases of mistaken identity. The shark is hunted by trophy hunters, mainly for its jaws and teeth, but it is now fully protected in several countries.

Shadows in the sea

Sharks are more threatened by people than people are by sharks. Some, like the sandbar shark, don't mature until they are 30 years old. Sharks have few pups, and may only reproduce every two to three years. When a population is fished out, it is slow to recover, which means that some

10 species are seriously endangered.

Q: Why are sharks' fins cut off their bodies?

A: Sharks' fins are first dried and then turned into an expensive, oriental shark fin soup. The industry is so profitable that some fishermen do not bother to keep the rest of the shark. They slice off the fins (known as "finning") and throw the still-living bodies back into the sea. The sharks either drown or starve to death.

Awesome facts
The sand tiger shark gives birth to only two babies at a time. During development, these two eat their other womb mates inside their mother's body.

The basking shark is caught for its liver oil, which is used to make cosmetics and to produce lubricating oil for high-flying aircraft. In the 1950s and 1960s, "baskers" off the Irish coast were overfished. Over 40 years later, scientists are still looking for signs that the population will recover.

Food from the sea

All over the world, fish that were once common are disappearing. Larger fish have been fished out first, and then gradually smaller individuals, until entire populations have crashed. Restrictions and quotas have been introduced to help restore stocks.

zoom in on...

Overfishing

Commercial fisheries have worked on a "boom-and-bust" principle. Huge quantities of fish are caught in one area during "boom" times. When stocks are depleted—the "bust" times—the fishing boats simply move elsewhere and start the destructive process all over again.

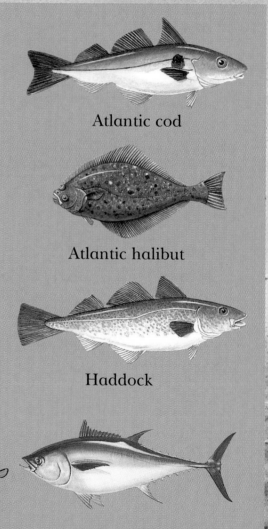

Atlantic cod

Atlantic halibut

Haddock

Bluefin tuna

In the Mediterranean, all the fishermen from a village sometimes join their boats and nets together to catch the magnificent bluefin tuna. The event is called *la mattanza*, which means "the killing." At one time, fishermen caught hundreds of tuna at a time, but today, they catch just a few because stocks have been overfished.

Q: Will there always be fish to eat?

A: Probably. Cod, halibut, and haddock—the fish that you often find in grocery stores—have all been overfished. However, similar white fish from the Southern Ocean, such as hoki, have yet to be exploited, so they could replace our usual cod or haddock.

Awesome facts

Mussels and other shellfish that have been in water invaded by "red tides" of venomous, floating red algae become poisonous and make the people that eat them sick.

Turtles and tortoises

Huge sea turtles swim to shore to lay their eggs on breeding beaches. Some islands have giant land tortoises living on them. Once, these islands were isolated and the reptiles safe, but when people arrived, they killed the tortoises and dug up their eggs for food.

zoom in on...

Turtle soup

Green turtles are the main ingredient of turtle soup. In the West Indies, green turtles were caught when they emerged to lay their eggs. One by one, each breeding population was destroyed. Today, some beaches are protected so that mother turtles can lay their eggs and the hatchlings can reach the sea safely.

If too many sea turtle eggs are taken, the turtle population collapses. Turtle-breeding beaches are also threatened by vacation resort developments. The noise and lights drive the turtles away and they cannot find anywhere to lay their eggs.

Green turtle

On Indian Ocean islands, such as Rodrigues, tortoises were turned upside down on their shells then stored alive on sailing ships to provide fresh meat for sailors. At one time, many Indian Ocean islands had tortoise populations, but by the early 1800s, most had been wiped out. Today, the only survivors live on the island of Aldabra.

Aldabra tortoise

Awesome facts

At over six feet long, the leatherback is the world's largest turtle. A female lays several clutches of eggs, with up to 170 eggs in each clutch, on a tropical beach.

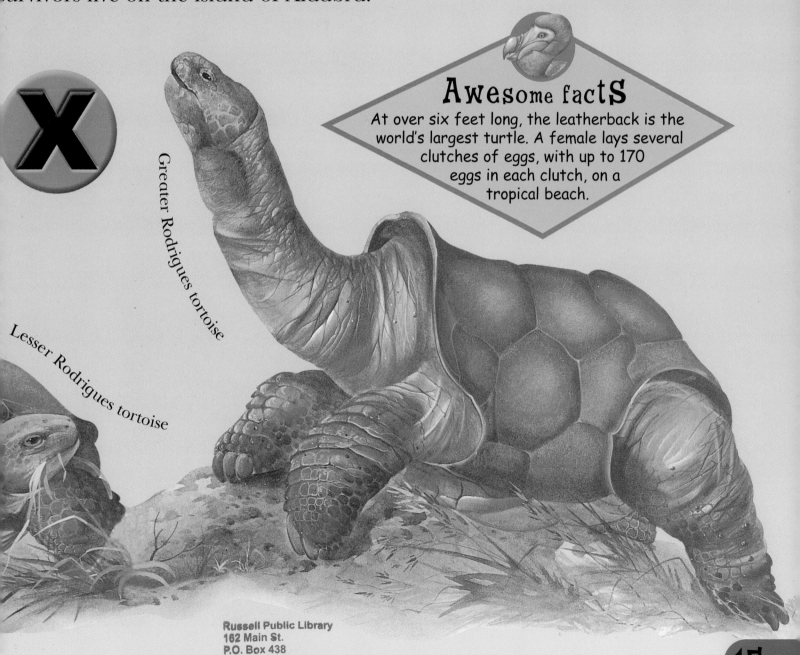

Greater Rodrigues tortoise

Lesser Rodrigues tortoise

zoom in on...

El Niño

The Galápagos Islands are usually bathed in cold water that sweeps up the South American coast from the Antarctic, but every four years or so, the currents reverse. This is known as El Niño. Warm water from the central Pacific pushes eastward past the islands. Fish head for deeper water. Seabirds abandon chicks because they cannot find food. Seals abandon their pups. Populations used to recover gradually, but now there are so few of some unique species left that they may become extinct.

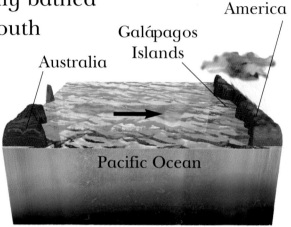

South America

Galápagos Islands

Australia

Pacific Ocean

In an El Niño year, strong currents and weak winds push warm water east toward South America.

Galápagos Islands

The Galápagos Islands in the Pacific Ocean were once a paradise for wildlife. Even today, the mammals, reptiles, and birds that live there do not run or fly away from people. It was these unique animals that helped Charles Darwin to work out his theory of evolution in the 1800s, but today, they are all under threat.

16

Awesome facts

"Charlie" is the only surviving giant tortoise on the Galápagos island of Abingdon. There are no females, so he is the last of his line with no chance to breed.

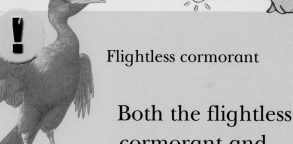

 Q: What threatens the wildlife of the Galápagos Islands?

A: Illegal fishing and shark fishing, introduced goats, cats, and rats, and the collection of sea cucumbers for the oriental market have all had a major impact on the survival of Galápagos wildlife. Irresponsible tourists and natural events, such as El Niño, have also affected them. But just one big oil spill could totally wipe out animals that live nowhere else in the world.

Flightless cormorant

Both the flightless cormorant and the marine iguana are unique to the Galápagos Islands. Both species are vulnerable to oil slicks because they rely on a clean and food-rich ocean. The cormorant dives below the surface to catch fish, and the iguana dives to graze on green seaweed from rocks near the shore.

Marine iguana

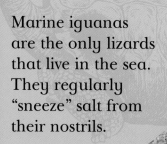

Marine iguanas are the only lizards that live in the sea. They regularly "sneeze" salt from their nostrils.

!

17

The sea mink was once found on the coasts of Canada and New England. It became a target for fur trappers, and the entire population was quickly wiped out. The last one was brought to a fur market in Jonesport, Maine, in 1880.

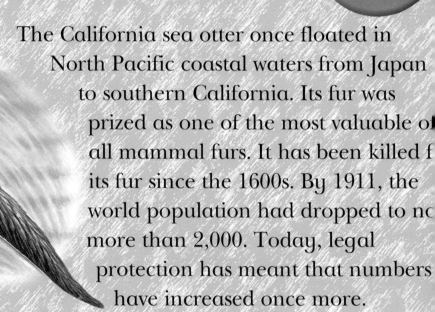

Sea mink

The California sea otter once floated in North Pacific coastal waters from Japan to southern California. Its fur was prized as one of the most valuable of all mammal furs. It has been killed f its fur since the 1600s. By 1911, the world population had dropped to no more than 2,000. Today, legal protection has meant that numbers have increased once more.

Sea otter

Mammals of the coast

For centuries, ferretlike animals, such as ermine and mink, have been hunted for their luxurious pelts, but the thicker, warmer fur of their seagoing relatives ha been even more desirable. Many have ended their days as expensive fur coats. Large-scale trapping ha caused some species to become extinct.

Q: Are fur coats necessary?

A: For ancient peoples living in cold climates, the only way to keep warm outside their homes was to wear clothes made from the pelts of animals with fur. These tribes lived in harmony with nature, taking only what was needed for survival. The commercial fur trappers and traders were different. They killed and sold as many animals as they could find, and had little regard for sustaining animal populations. They wiped out one species and then moved on to another.

Awesome factS

The sea otter uses tools. It floats on its back, places a large stone on its belly, and smashes shellfish and sea urchins against it, to break them and eat the soft parts inside.

Q: How do we know what extinct animals looked like?

A: Mainly through skeletons, fossils, and stuffed and mounted bodies. For example, Steller's spectacled cormorant (right) is only known to the scientific community through six stuffed specimens and two skeletons. Just one scientist, Georg Steller, saw these slow-moving birds alive, before they were all caught by whalers and sealers in the North Pacific. They were extinct by 1850.

Up to the 900s, there were tens of millions of flightless great auks nesting on North Atlantic islands. They were caught for food and their feathers were used to stuff pillows. The last pair was clubbed to death and the egg smashed when three fishermen arrived on Eldey Island, off the Iceland coast, on June 3, 1844.

Great auks

20

Seabirds

Auks are the northern hemisphere equivalent of penguins. They dive for food, using their wings like flippers. One species, the great auk, lost the power of flight completely. When early explorers came along, the birds were vulnerable, and were easily caught.

Wandering albatross populations have declined by 30 percent. This is partly because the fish and squid they eat are vanishing due to overfishing. Adult birds also follow fishing boats in the Southern Ocean and many drown when they get caught on fishing hooks.

Awesome facts

Discarded fishing nets, known as "ghost nets," frequently catch birds and other animals by mistake. Their victims are often seabirds, such as auks and penguins.

21

The elephant bird of Madagascar weighed nearly 1,000 pounds (450 kg), making it the world's largest bird at the time it lived. It also laid the largest egg of any bird, living or dead. Its eggs were brought back to Europe by sailors in the 1500s. Egg collecting, hunting, and destruction of its forest home ensured the species would not survive. By about 1700, it was extinct.

Awesome facts

The elephant bird was thought to be the "roc-bird," described by Marco Polo in 1298, and also the legendary "roc" in the stories of Sinbad.

Island giants

Animals in isolation, such as those on islands, tend to become overspecialized. Some grow very large. Birds are no exception, and on some islands there were once real giants. When humans came along, they considered the birds to be food and hunted them. The giant birds were so large that there were few places to hide and they quickly became extinct.

In New Zealand, the giant moa and its relatives once grew to a height of 13 feet (4 m). In the 900s, the Maoris arrived from Polynesia and hunted the moas for food. The last is thought to have died about 100 years before Captain Cook visited the islands in the 1700s.

Maori

X

Dodo

"As dead as a dodo" refers to the extermination of a strangely shaped flightless pigeon that once lived on the Indian Ocean island of Mauritius. It was a foul-tasting bird, yet it was clubbed to death for sport, and its eggs were eaten by introduced cats, rats, pigs, and monkeys. The dodo was extinct by 1680. On the nearby island of Rodrigues, the solitaire (below) went the same way 100 years later. Solitaires had a large knob on each wing with which they could hit attackers.

Dodo tree

Since the dodo died out, not one dodo tree sapling has grown in the wild, despite existing trees bearing fruit and seeds. The seeds need to pass through a dodo's stomach before they can sprout and grow, so no dodo means no new trees. Turkeys have now been fed the seeds and their droppings collected. As a result, the first new dodo trees for 300 years have started to grow.

Until recently, there were only about 20 Mauritius pink pigeons left. A captive breeding program has now increased numbers by raising birds in captivity and returning them to the wild.

The pigeon hollandaise was a crested pigeon from Mauritius. It tasted good and was shot for food. Introduced monkeys ate its eggs and the species was extinct by 1826.

Odd pigeons

The pigeon family has been successful all over the world. On islands such as Mauritius, some species evolved into bizarre shapes and sizes. With few ground predators, they lost the ability to fly. This left them especially helpless when people landed on their islands.

When a lighthouse was put up on Stephen's Island, New Zealand, the keeper brought his cat with him. The cat caught the island's wrens. These birds were found nowhere else in the world, and their skins fetched premium prices in museums. But the cat caught the entire population and the Stephen's Island wren was discovered and exterminated in the same year: 1894.

Q: Why do so many island birds die out?

A: Any introduced animals threaten island birds. When people land on islands, they bring mammals, such as rats, cats, dogs, pigs, and goats, with them. These kill the island animals or destroy the plants on which they feed or in which they hide.

Island birds

Islands tend to have few mammal predators. Without the need to flee danger on the ground, many island birds have become flightless. This puts them at a disadvantage, however, when any mammals do arrive.

The world's largest parrot is the kakapo, a flightless ground-living parrot from New Zealand. Its decline is due to introduced rats that eat its eggs and chicks. A few birds have been captured and moved to rat-free islands, where it is hoped they will reproduce and restore the population.

The Mauritius kestrel is considered to be one of the rarest birds in the world. It was shot by islanders because it raided chicken coops. In 1973, there were just nine kestrels left, but a captive breeding program has released 250 young birds to help boost numbers.

Stephen's Island wren

Apapane

Honeycreepers

These birds became so specialized that they were unable to adapt when humans arrived with their domestic animals and diseases. Introduced pigs, cattle, and deer upset the plant life, and many birds caught diseases like avian malaria. This was introduced in 1826, when a ship accidentally introduced the mosquitoes that carry the disease. Every bird living in the lowlands died, and 40 percent of species disappeared.

Hawaiian akioloa

Several species of honeyeaters, also called O-Os, became extinct between 1837 and 1934. They were first collected to provide feathers for the traditional capes worn by Hawaiian chiefs. Then, 50 percent of island plant life was destroyed by fire and by cattle brought in by European settlers. Introduced pests, such as cats and rats, were the last straw.

Molokai O-O

zoom in on...

Oahu O-O

The hoary bat is Hawaii's only native mammal. It is threatened by the large-scale removal of the forests in which it lives, and by the use of pesticides, which has reduced the amount of available insect food.

Hawaiian O-O

Hawaii

Isolated in the middle of the Pacific Ocean, the wildlife of the Hawaiian islands evolved into many specialized species found nowhere else in the world. Two bird groups, honeyeaters and honeycreepers, took specialization to an extreme: the shape of their bills became adapted for different kinds of food.

Back from the dead

Many small, remote islands have not been studied carefully. Occasionally, animals and plants thought to be extinct on large islands have been rediscovered on their smaller neighbors. In some cases, all a species needs to survive is a single rocky pinnacle sticking out of the sea, undisturbed by people or domestic animals.

 Q: Who decides when an animal is endangered?

A: The IUCN (International Union for the Conservation of Nature and Natural Resources) coordinates research about surviving plant and animal families. The status of each species is assessed and the findings are published in Red Data Books. The buying, selling, hunting, and poaching of wild animals is monitored by CITES (Convention on International Trade in Endangered Species of Wild Fauna and Flora).

Lord Howe Island stick insects are also known as land lobsters. They disappeared about 80 years ago, but in February 2001, a group of Australian scientists rediscovered a colony, not on the main island, but on a tiny rock pinnacle called Balls Pyramid, 14 miles (23 km) to the southeast.

Glossary

blubber
The thick layer of fat under the skin of most sea mammals which helps to keep them warm.

captive breeding
The breeding of animals in zoos and parks to preserve endangered species.

endangered
Describes a species which is likely to die out if the factors causing its decline continue.

evolution
The process by which all plants and animals appeared, how they developed over time, and how they are still changing gradually today.

extinct
Describes a species that has not been seen in the wild for 50 years or more.

fossil
The remains of any ancient plant or animal, usually preserved in rock.

habitat
The place where an animal lives, usually characterized by the plants that grow there.

hatchling
A baby bird or reptile that has just emerged from an egg.

inshore waters
Shallow waters near the coast.

introduced
Describes a species brought by humans into a habitat where it does not occur naturally.

mammal
A backboned animal with hair, like a cat or human, which feeds its young on milk.

oil slick
A film of oil on the surface of the sea that has escaped from an oil tanker or terminal.

overfishing
The catching of too many fish, which may cause a fish population to disappear.

pesticide
A poisonous chemical used to kill plants and animals that are considered to be pests.

pollution
Damage caused to an area by chemical or biological materials, including oil, sewage, and industrial waste.

population
A group of individuals of the same type.

predator
An animal that hunts and eats other animals.

quota
A certain allowed quantity.

reptile
A backboned animal with scales that lays eggs, such as a crocodile.

sealers
People who hunt seals.

species
A group of animals that resemble each other and are able to breed together.

whalers
People who hunt whales.

31

Index